Best Kids' Halloween Jokes EVER!

Highlights Press
Honesdale, Pennsylvania

Cover art by Neil Numberman
Contributing Illustrators: Paula Becker, David Coulson, Mike Dammer,
Kelly Kennedy, Pat Lewis, Mike Moran, Neil Numberman, Jim Paillot,
Rich Powell, Keven Rechin, Rick Stromoski, Pete Whitehead

Published by Highlights for Children
815 Church Street
Honesdale, Pennsylvania 18431
Printed in Mattoon, IL, USA

ISBN: 978-1-64472-119-3
First edition

Visit our website at Highlights.com.

10 9 8 7 6 5 4 3 2 1

CONTENTS

PUNNY PUMPKINS

Why is Cinderella so bad at sports?

Because she has a pumpkin for a coach and runs away from the ball.

What did the pumpkin patch say to the farmer?

"Quit picking on me."

Why did the jack-o'-lantern go to school?

He wanted to get brighter.

What do you call a pretty pumpkin?

Gourd-geous

Knock, knock.

Who's there?

Pumpkin.

Pumpkin who?

A pumpkin fill up your flat tire.

Jamie: I've been working on a magic trick.

Grace: What kind?

Jamie: You throw a pumpkin up in the air, and it comes down squash!

Why was the jack-o'-lantern afraid to cross the road?

It had no guts.

Why were the two pumpkins so close?

They had deep roots.

What do you call a pile of pumpkins?

A stack-o'-lanterns

Why do jack-o'-lanterns admire scarecrows?

They have been looking up to them since they were pumpkins.

What do Hawaiian pumpkins say?

"Happy Hula-ween!"

What did one pumpkin say to the other?

"I'm vine, thanks for asking."

What do you get when you divide the circumference of a jack-o'-lantern by its diameter?

Pumpkin pi

Why do pumpkins sit on people's porches?

They can't knock on the door.

How do you fix a jack-o'-lantern?

With a pumpkin patch

What did one jack-o'-lantern say to the other?

"Why don't you lighten up?"

Who helps little pumpkins cross the road safely?

The crossing gourd

Where do you find the most famous jack-o'-lanterns?

In the Hall of Flame

Two pumpkin pies are sitting in an oven.

Pie 1: Does it feel warm in here to you?

Pie 2: AAH! A talking pie!

What do you get when you cross a pumpkin and a duck?

A quack-o'-lantern

Who is the leader of all jack-o'-lanterns?

The Pumpking

What did the orange pumpkin say to the green pumpkin?

"Why orange you orange?"

How do gourds get to be so strong?

By pumpkin iron

What does a pumpkin pie say after a big meal?

"That was filling."

What do you call an athletic pumpkin?

A jock-o'-lantern

Knock, knock.

Who's there?

Dispatch.

Dispatch who?

Dispatch of pumpkins is huge!

What did the jack-o'-lantern say to the pumpkin?

"Cut it out!"

What's the best thing to put in a pumpkin pie?

Your teeth

If you eat two-thirds of a pumpkin pie, what do you have?

An angry mom

GOOFY GHOSTS

Ted: I didn't know our school was haunted.

Ned: Neither did I. How did you find out?

Ted: Everybody's been talking about our school spirit!

When does a ghost's work week start?

On Moan-day

Why do ghosts and demons get along?

Because demons are a ghoul's best friend

Knock, knock.

Who's there?

Zelda.

Zelda who?

Zelda house, I think it's haunted!

What kind of horse does the boogeyman ride?

A nightmare

Why are graveyards so noisy?

Because of all the coffin

How does a ghost offer tea?

With scream or sugar

Where do baby ghosts go when their parents are at work?

The day-scare center

What do you get when you cross a ghost and a bird?

The grim cheeper

How do ghosts like to travel?

On scare-planes

What did one ghost say to the other ghost?

"Do you believe in people?"

What type of pants do ghosts wear?

Boo jeans

Why did the policeman ticket the ghost on Halloween?

It didn't have a haunting license.

What kind of ghost has the best hearing?

The eeriest

What is a ghost's favorite drink?

Ghoul-Aid

What kind of mistakes do ghosts make?

Boo-boos

Nurse: Doctor, there's a ghost in the waiting room.

Doctor: Tell him I can't see him.

Which kind of ghost haunts a chicken coop?

A poultry-geist

How did the little ghost learn to play the piano?

By using sheet music

What do you call a ghost's mother and father?

Transparents

Where do ghosts play golf?

On a golf corpse

Who writes books about haunted houses?

Ghostwriters

Why do ghosts make good cheerleaders?

Because they have a lot of spirit

When does a ghost have breakfast?

In the moan-ing

What did the ghost teacher say to the class?

"Look at the board and I will go through it again."

What plants like Halloween the most?

Bamboo

How do ghosts keep fit?

By exorcising regularly

What do you call a ghost with no nose or body?

Nobodynose

What do ghosts drink?

Evaporated milk

What did one ghost say to the other?

"It's fa-boo-lous to see you!"

Why don't ghosts like rain on Halloween?

It dampens their spirits.

Knock, knock.

Who's there?

Dancer.

Dancer who?

Dancer is simple; it wasn't a ghost—it was only the wind!

What is a ghost's favorite position in soccer?

Ghoul-keeper

Where's the best place to build a haunted house?

A dead-end street

What is a phantom's favorite ride at the amusement park?

The roller ghoster

What do ghosts eat for dinner?

Ghoulash

Why don't ghosts tell lies?

Because you can see right through them

Where do ghosts mail letters?

The ghost office

What's a ghost's favorite meal?

Spook-etti

What do ghosts say on April 1st?

"April Ghouls!"

Why did the ghost starch his sheet?

He wanted everyone to be scared stiff.

What do ghosts wash their hair with?

Sham-boo

Which three letters would surprise a ghost?

I C U

What is a ghost's favorite day of the week?

Fright-day

What do ghosts eat for breakfast?

Scream of wheat

**What baseball team does
a ghost like best?**

The Boo York Yankees

What does a ghost do to stay safe in a car?

Put on a sheet belt

Knock, knock.

Who's there?

Zone.

Zone who?

**He's scared of his zone
shadow.**

What's a ghost's favorite musical?

Phantom of the Opera

What do you call a prehistoric ghost?

A terror-dactyl

What's white, black, and blue all over?

A ghost that can't go through walls

Where do ghosts take a cruise?

The Boo-hamas

What kind of ghosts haunt skyscrapers?

High spirits

Teacher: Where is your homework?

Boy: A ghost ate it.

Teacher: I can see right through that excuse!

What is a ghost's favorite fruit?

Boo-berries

What room does a ghost not need in her house?

A living room

Where do ghosts like to go for dinner?

To a resta-haunt

What happens when a ghost gets lost in a fog?

He is mist.

What is a ghost's favorite bedtime story?

Little Boo Peep

What's a ghost's favorite lake?

Lake Eerie

What do baby ghosts wear on their feet?

Bootees

What do you call a phantom by a campfire?

A toasty ghosty

What do ghosts do at garage sales?

They go bargain haunting.

Knock, knock.

Who's there?

Ghost.

Ghost who?

Ghost to show you don't remember my name!

Where do ghosts buy their milk and eggs?

At the ghost-ery store

What do ghosts with bad eyesight wear?

Spook-tacles

Why did the ghost get kicked out of the football game?

Because he screamed, "Boo!"

What's a ghost's favorite carnival ride?

The scary-go-round

What did the little ghost give her mom for Mother's Day?

A boo-quet of flowers

Why do ghosts like to ride in elevators?

It raises their spirits.

ZANY ZOMBIES

Knock, knock.

Who's there?

Zombies.

Zombies who?

Only zom-bees in a hive make honey.

**Why did the zombie comedian
get booed off the stage?**

*Because the jokes he told
were rotten*

What can't a zombie eat for breakfast?

Lunch and dinner

**Did you hear about the
zombie Halloween party?**

It was a scream.

Why did the zombie do so well on his exam?

Because it was a no-brainer

Knock, knock.

Who's there?

Crypt

Crypt who?

She crypt up behind me.

How do zombies tell their futures?

With a horror-scope

What's a zombie's favorite part of a hockey game?

The zomb-oni

Why don't zombies eat comedians?

They taste funny.

What do vegetarian zombies crave?

Graaaains

When do zombies go to sleep?

When they are dead tired

What do zombies like to eat at barbecues?

Hallo-weenies

Ji-hye: Is it true that a zombie won't attack you if you're carrying a flashlight?

Hae-won: It depends on how fast you're carrying the flashlight!

What do you call a bee that never dies?

A zom-bee

What did the zombie's mom do when she got mad at him?

She grounded him.

Why did the zombie eat brains?

She wanted food for thought.

Pretend it's Halloween and a zombie is chasing you. What do you do?

Stop pretending!

What did one zombie say to the other?

"Get a life."

Why didn't the zombie go to school?

He felt rotten.

What is a zombie's favorite sauce to have with brains?

Grave-y

Knock, knock.

Who's there?

Voodoo.

Voodoo who?

Voodoo you think you are?

Why do zombies like scientists?

They're always brainstorming.

Nick: Did you hear the joke about the zombie?

Reese: No, tell me.

Nick: Never mind, it takes brains.

How does a zombie greet someone?

"Pleased to eat you!"

Why did the zombie become a comedian?

He wanted to make people laugh their heads off.

WACKY WITCHES

Why didn't the witch sing at the concert?

She had a frog in her throat.

What do witches put on their bagels?

Scream cheese

How do you make a witch itch?

Take away the W.

Why do witches make such good gardeners?

They have green thumbs.

What do you call a wizard from outer space?

A flying sorcerer

What does a witch request at a hotel?

Broom service

What is a witch's favorite subject?

Spelling

What is the difference between a witch and the letters M-A-K-E-S?

One makes spells and the others spell makes.

What does a witch use to keep her hair up?

Scare-spray

Why did the witch paint her toenails orange?

So she could hide in the pumpkin patch

How do witches tell the time?

By looking at their witch-watches.

What did one witch say to the other before the spelling bee?

"Witch me luck!"

What's a wizard's favorite sport?

Tae kWAND do

Why did the witch fall in love with the janitor?

Because he swept her off her feet

Where do witches get their hair done?

The ugly parlor

What do you call a witch's garage?

A broom closet

What's the first thing witches do on Halloween morning?

They wake up.

Knock, knock.

Who's there?

Witches.

Witches who?

Witches the way to go home?

33

Spencer: Have you heard the joke about the witch's broom?

Phil: No, I haven't.

Spencer: It's sweeping the nation.

When is it bad luck to see a witch's cat?

When you're a mouse

What do you get if you cross a dinosaur with a wizard?

Tyrannosaurus hex

What does a broom do when it's tired?

It goes to sweep.

What do you call a witch who likes the beach but is scared of the water?

A chicken sand-witch

How many witches does it take to change a light bulb?

Just one, but she changes it into a toad.

What kind of tests do they give in witch school?

Hex-aminations

Who turns the lights off on Halloween?

The light's witch

Where do wizards keep their teacups?

On sorcerers

What goes *cackle, cackle, bonk*?

A witch laughing her head off

What do you call two witches who share the same room?

Broommates

What did the wizard say to his girlfriend?

"You look wand-erful tonight."

What do you get if you cross a witch and an iceberg?

A cold spell

How do witches fly when their broomsticks are broken?

On spell-icopters

What kind of writing does a witch use?

Cursive

Why did the witch go to the doctor?

Because she has a dizzy spell

What do witches love about their computers?

The spell-checker

How do you make a witch float?

With two scoops of ice cream, a bottle of root beer, and a witch

What do witches race on?

Vroomsticks

What kind of makeup do witches wear?

Mas-scare-a

Knock, knock.

Who's there?

Leaf.

Leaf who?

**Leaf me alone—
I'm practicing
my spells.**

**Why did the witch put
her broom in the washing
machine?**

*She wanted a clean
sweep.*

What does a witch's cat like for breakfast?

Mice crispies

**What did one broom say to
the other broom at bedtime?**

"Sweep tight."

Samantha: Did you hear the joke about the
witch?

Nicole: No, tell me.

Samantha: Be careful what you witch for!

Why do witches always wear name tags?

So you can tell which witch is which

What sounds do a witch's cereal make?

Snap, cackle, and pop

Where do witches go to wash their clothes?

The laundry broom

What's a witch's favorite hobby?

Arts and witchcrafts

Knock, knock.

Who's there?

Spell.

Spell who?

W-H-O.

MONSTER MIRTH

Julia: Mom! There's a monster under my bed!

Mom: Tell him to get back in the closet where he belongs.

Why did Frankenstein's monster like the stand-up comic?

Because she kept him in stitches

How does a monster count to 23?

On its fingers

Knock, knock.

Who's there?

Ogre.

Ogre who?

Please do it ogre again.

How did newspapers describe the day Frankenstein's monster was created?

They said it was shocking.

How do you keep a monster from smelling?

Hold its nose.

What is a monster's favorite dessert?

I scream

Teacher: Why didn't you finish your homework?

Monster: I was full.

What did the critics say about the ogre's piece of art?

"What a monster-piece!"

What do you call a monster with a lot of children?

A Mom-ster

What do monsters put on before they go in the pool?

Sun-scream

Knock, knock.

Who's there?

Thumping.

Thumping who?

Thumping green and thlimy is crawling up your leg.

What is a monster's favorite game?

Swallow the leader

Girl Monster: Mom, the teacher said I was nice, smart, and well-behaved.

Mother Monster: Don't feel bad, dear. You'll do better next semester.

Knock, knock.

Who's there?

Juicy.

Juicy who?

Juicy any monsters under my bed?

What should you do if a monster rolls his eyes at you?

Roll the eyes back to him.

What's the best way to talk to a monster?

Long distance

What do you call a monster with no neck?

The Lost Neck Monster

Monster 1: Have you ever tried to eat a clock?

Monster 2: No, it would be too time-consuming.

What do you do with a green monster?

Wait until it ripens.

What is a monster's favorite kind of cheese?

Monsterella

Who did the troll take to the dance?

His ghoul friend

Who is the best dancer at a monster party?

The boogie-man

Stuart: Have you heard the joke about the monster?

John: No.

Stuart: Never mind—it stinks.

Why did the monster's mother knit him three socks for Halloween?

She heard he grew another foot.

Knock, knock.

Who's there?

Weaver.

Weaver who?

Weaver alone, you mean monster!

What do you get when you cross a monster and an inventor?

Benjamin Franklinstein

Where do monsters go to college?

At goon-iversities

Who won the monster beauty contest?

Nobody

Why did the monster need braces?

Because he had an ogre-bite

Danny: What do you call a monster wearing earmuffs?

Doug: I don't know. What?

Danny: It doesn't matter. He can't hear you.

What do you call rotten eggs, rotten fruit, and spoiled milk in a bag?

Gross-eries

How do you greet a three-headed monster?

"Hello, hello, hello!"

Why wasn't Dr. Frankenstein ever lonely?

Because he was so good at making new friends.

First Monster: We must be getting close to a city.

Second Monster: How can you tell?

First Monster: We're stepping on more cars.

CRUSH! SMASH! CRUNCH!

What did the monster say to his mother when he slept through his alarm?

Sorry, I ogre-slept!

What does a sea monster eat for dinner?

Fish and ships

When a monster puts his tooth under his pillow, who comes to get it?

The tooth scary

Knock, knock.

Who's there?

Scurry.

Scurry who?

Scurry monsters live in the swamp!

Why did the cyclops stop teaching?

Because he only had one pupil

What did the people say when the goo monsters attacked?

"Ooze going to save us?"

What has 8 legs, 9 eyes, and 20 hands?

I don't know, but it's crawling up your leg!

Who is the smartest monster?

Frank Einstein

Knock, knock.

Who's there?

Eliza.

Eliza who?

Eliza wake at night thinking about monsters his brother drew.

Why did the monster eat the light bulb?

Because he wanted a light snack

Who went into the monster's lair and came out alive?

The monster

What do you call a clean, neat, hardworking, kind, intelligent monster?

A failure

HILARIOUS HARVEST

What do you call people who like tractors?

Protractors

Ma: Don't order those seeds. It says they won't be ready until next fall.

Pa: That's OK. This is last year's catalog.

Why don't scarecrows eat?

They're already stuffed.

What did the mare say when she finished her hay?

"That's the last straw."

Why did the farmer cross the road?

To bring back his chicken

What is a scarecrow's favorite fruit?

Straw-berries

What did one leaf say to the other?

"Have a nice fall."

Why can't you tell a secret in a cornfield?

There are too many ears.

What is a scarecrow's favorite food?

Stuffing

Scarecrow: What's wrong with me, Doctor?

Doctor: Well, it looks like you might have hay fever.

Why did the scarecrow win a prize?

He was outstanding in his field.

Why did the farmer plant cranberries on the road?

He wanted cranberry juice.

Knock, knock.

Who's there?

Ear.

Ear who?

Ear you are. I've been looking everywhere!

What did the corn maze say when the scarecrow gave it a compliment?

"Aw shucks, thanks."

Why did the girl take a bale of hay to bed with her?

To feed her nightmare

Donnie: My grandfather made a scarecrow so scary that it scared every crow off our farm.

Luisa: You think that's something? I made one so scary that the crows brought back the corn they took last year.

What do scarecrows do at bedtime?

They hit the hay.

Knock, knock.

Who's there?

Ears.

Ears who?

Ears looking at you, kid.

What's a scarecrow's favorite crop?

Beets me!

How does a scarecrow drink his juice?

With a straw

What did the scarecrow say to the cornstalk on Halloween?

"Your costume is a-maize-ing."

Kid: I'd be surprised if you got 10 pounds of apples from that tree.

Farmer: So would I. It's a pear tree.

CRAZY COSTUMES

Knock, knock.

Who's there?

Dragon.

Dragon who?

Dragon easy chair over here and let's talk about our costumes.

What do you get when a dinosaur dresses up like a football player for Halloween?

A quarterback no one can tackle

Why did the pig want to be an actor for Halloween?

He was a big ham.

A duck walks into a costume store. He buys a Halloween costume.

Cashier: How would you like to pay?

Duck: Put it on my bill.

Why is Superman's costume so tight?

Because he wears a size "S"

What do you get when a shark dresses up like a U.S. president for Halloween?

Jaws Washington

Knock, knock.

Who's there?

Defeat.

Defeat who?

**Defeat are hurting in this costume.
Can I sit down?**

Dad: What was that loud noise?

Hari: My Halloween costume fell on the floor.

Dad: Why would your Halloween costume falling make such a loud noise?

Hari: Because I was wearing it.

Knock, knock.

Who's there?

Cow.

Cow who?

Cow much do you like our costumes?

What do you call a *Tyrannosaurus rex* when it dresses like a cowboy for Halloween?

Tyrannosaurus tex

Knock, knock.

Who's there?

Interrupting pirate.

Interrupting pirate. Who?

Interrupting pir—ARRRRRRR!

Why do leaves change colors before Halloween?

Because they want to get their costumes ready

Who always dresses like a king for Halloween?

The ruler

Knock, knock.

Who's there?

Howl.

Howl who?

Howl you be dressing up for Halloween this year?

What do you call a person wearing an alphabet suit for Halloween?

A letter carrier

Knock, knock.

Who's there?

Disguise.

Disguise who?

Disguise the limit!

How did the grandmother knit a suit of armor for her grandson's costume?

She used steel wool.

Knock, knock.

Who's there?

Geometry.

Geometry who?

Geometry for Halloween, but I wish I were a flower.

Knock, knock.

Who's there?

Mister E.

Mister E. who?

Mister E. meat is what they're serving on Halloween.

SILLY SKELETONS

Why was the skeleton afraid of the dog?

The dog wanted to take his bones.

What do you call a tired skeleton on Halloween?

The grim sleeper

Why was the skeleton so serious?

His funny bone was missing.

Where do skeletons go to class?

Elementary skull

What is a skeleton's favorite plant?

A bone-zai tree

Why don't skeletons play music in church?

They have no organs.

What do you call a skeleton snake?

A rattler

Which skeleton declared himself emperor?

Napoleon Bone-aparte

Why didn't the skeleton like candy?

He didn't have the stomach for it.

What do you call a skeleton who uses the doorbell?

A dead ringer

What do skeletons say on Halloween?

"Crick or creak!"

What is a skeleton's favorite instrument?

A trombone

What do you call a skeleton that is always telling lies?

A bony phony

What do you do if you see a skeleton running across the road?

Jump out of your skin and join him!

Why did the skeleton laugh at the joke?

Because he thought it was humerus

How do skeletons get their mail?

By bony express

Why are skeletons so calm, cool, and collected?

Because nothing gets under their skin

What do you call a skeleton who loves to clean?

The grim sweeper

What kind of plates do skeletons eat on?

Bone china

Why did the skeleton cross the road?

To get to the body shop

How do you greet a French skeleton?

"Bone-jour."

How did the skeleton know it was going to rain on Halloween?

He could feel it in his bones.

Why didn't the skeleton like recess?

She had no body to play with.

What did the skeleton bring to the Halloween party?

Spare ribs

Who was the most famous skeleton detective?

Sherlock Bones

What has 1854 bones and catches flies?

A skeleton baseball team

Doctor: You need new eyeglasses.

Patient: How can you tell?

Doctor: You're talking to my skeleton model. I'm over here.

Why don't skeletons work as stunt men?

They don't have the guts.

What is a skeleton's favorite fruit?

Spine-apples

What do you call a lie told by a skeleton?

A little fib-ula

How do skeletons call their friends?

On the tele-bone

What do you call a skeleton who can't stop crying?

The grim weeper

What song do skeleton bikers ride to?

"Bone to Be Wild"

Skeleton: I've been asked to be in a play.

Body: Did you say yes?

Skeleton: No way! Who wants to be in a cast?

Why did the skeleton do extra homework?

Because he wanted the bone-us points

What do skeletons send each other on Halloween?

Scare packages

Why did the skeleton go to the library?

She was boning up for her exams.

Why do skeletons get sick on windy days?

The wind goes right through them.

Why did the skeleton always tell the truth?

He wanted tibia honest.

What do you get when you cross a pig with a skeleton?

A pork-u-spine

MUMMY MANIA

What is a mummy's favorite sport?

Casket-ball

What promise do Egyptian funeral directors make?

Satisfaction guaranteed or your mummy back.

Why did King Tut have a hard time making friends?

Because he was all wrapped up in himself

Why did the mummy go to the doctor?

He had a mummy-ache.

What's a mummy's favorite meal?

Chicken wraps

Where do mummies go on vacation?

The Dead Sea

What do mummies take when they are sick?

Coffin drops

Why couldn't mummies read emails inside their tombs?

They were in-crypt-ed.

Why do mummies love Halloween?

Because of all the free candy wrappers

Why did people go to see the stand-up comedian mummy?

His impressions were dead on.

What kind of jewels do mummies wear?

Tombstones

What do you call a very, very, very old joke?

Pre-hysterical

Why did the Egyptian cross the road?

Because he wanted to see his mummy

Why was the mummy upset?

She made a grave error.

What was the mummy rock band documentary about?

Their band aging

How do mummies hide?

They wear masking tape.

Where did cats get buried in ancient Egypt?

In purr-amids

What do you do when you see a mummy with a soccer ball?

Get out of the way!

Which mummy could jump higher than a pyramid?

All of them. Pyramids can't jump.

Where do pharaohs like to eat?

Pizza Tut

What did the director say when she finished filming a mummy scene?

"That's a wrap!"

What do you get when you cross a magician and a mummy?

Abra-cadaver

How did the mummy's secretary answer her calls?

"She can't talk right now—she's all wrapped up."

Why are mummies bad at giving directions?

They always lead to dead ends.

Why didn't the mummy want to go home after vacation?

Because he was in de-Nile

How do mummy baseball games always end?

In a tie

Do you want to hear a joke about building the pyramids?

I'm still working on it.

What's the most popular holiday in ancient Egypt?

Mummy's Day

How do you use an ancient Egyptian doorbell?

Toot-and-come-in!

Where do mummies go when their back hurts?

To a Cairo-practor

What is a mummy's favorite game?

Name that Tomb

How do you find out a mummy's age?

You go to her birthday party.

Why do mummies make good spies?

They're good at keeping things under wraps.

How many blocks did the Egyptian need to finish the pyramid?

Just the last one

What do you call a giant mummy?

Gauzilla

Why do mummies never trust a sphinx?

They're partly lion.

How is a mummy like a clock?

They're both wound up.

Why did the mom go to the Halloween party?

So she could dress like a mummy

What do you get in a five-star pyramid?

A tomb with a view

Jaxon: Want to hear a mummy joke?

Andi: Sure!

Jaxon: Never mind, it sphinx.

What's the best place to build a pyramid?

On a dead-end street

What do mummies use to take their temperature?

A ther-mummy-ter

What is a mummy's favorite ice cream?

Sphinx Tracks

Why was the mummy afraid to go to the library?

Because his books were thousands of years overdue

How is a mummy like a birthday gift?

Both are wrapped

What did the pharaoh say when he saw the pyramid?

"Mummy's home!"

Why don't mummies like to take vacations?

They're afraid to relax and unwind.

What's a mummy's favorite soup?

Cream of Tomb-ato

Where is a mummy cat when the lights go out?

In the dark

What did King Tut say when he was scared?

"I want my mummy."

What is a mummy's favorite type of music?

Wrap

Why did the mummy climb to the top of the pyramid to sing?

She wanted to reach the high notes.

What did one pyramid say to the other?

"How's your mummy?"

How do mummies say good-bye?

"See you tomb-orrow!"

VEXING VAMPIRES

What is a vampire's favorite animal?

A giraffe

How did the vampire invite his friend to dinner?

"Let's go out for a bite."

What is a vampire's favorite fruit?

A blood orange

What do you get when you cross a snowman with a vampire?

Frostbite

Why does the vampire consider himself a good artist?

Because he likes to draw blood

Where does a vampire get all her jokes?

From a crypt writer

What does a vampire stand on after taking a shower?

A bat mat

What do you call a vampire that lives in a kitchen?

Count Spatula

Why do vampires need mouthwash?

Because they have bat breath

What do you call a duck with fangs?

Quackula

Knock, knock.

Who's there?

Vampire.

Vampire who?

The Vampire State Building.

How can you tell when a vampire has been in a bakery?

All the jelly has been sucked out of the jelly doughnuts.

What is a vampire's favorite holiday?

Fangs-giving

Why did the vampire keep falling for the oldest tricks in the book?

Because he's a sucker

What type of dog does every vampire have?

Bloodhound

What would you get if you crossed a vampire and a teacher?

Lots of blood tests

Which flavor of ice cream is Dracula's favorite?

Vein-illa

How can you tell a vampire likes baseball?

Every night he turns into a bat.

What kind of bad dreams do vampires have?

Bite-mares

Why did the vampire give up acting?

He couldn't sink his teeth into the part.

What's a vampire's favorite dance?

The fang-dango

How does a vampire start a letter?

Tomb it may concern

Why did Dracula go to the doctor?

He was coffin.

What is a vampire's favorite circus act?

He always goes for the juggler!

How did the vampire fall in love with his wife?

It was love at first bite.

What has fangs, wears a cape, and lives underwater?

A clam-pire

Why don't vampires have any friends?

Because they're a pain in the neck

What is a vampire's favorite food?

A neck-tarine

What do you get when you cross a vampire and a computer?

A megabite

What do vampires wear on the first day of school?

Their bat-to-school clothes

Where do vampires go on vacation?

Pennsyl-vein-ia

What is Dracula's favorite coffee?

De-coffin-ated

Why did the vampire go to the dentist?

To improve his bite

What kind of mail do famous vampires get?

Fang mail

Divya: Did you hear about the race between the two vampires?

Nadia: I heard it was neck and neck!

Why did the vampire become a vegetarian?

He heard stake was bad for his heart.

What animal has fangs and webbed feet?

Count Duckula

Why did the vampire drive on the motorway?

Someone told him it was a main artery.

What's a vampire's favorite soup?

Scream of mushroom

Knock, knock.

Who's there?

Fangs.

Fangs who?

Fangs for letting me in.

Why are vampires good people to take out . . .?

Because they eat necks to nothing

What song do vampires hate?

You Are My Sunshine

What is a vampire's favorite game?

Tooth or scare

What do you get if you cross Dracula and Al Capone?

A fang-ster

Why did the vampire get in trouble with his dad?

Because he had a bat attitude

Where do vampires keep their money?

The blood bank

What's the best way to prevent infection from biting vampires?

Don't bite them.

CANDY CHUCKLES

What is a fish's favorite Halloween candy?

Bubble gum

Why did the boy put candy under his pillow?

Because he wanted sweet dreams

What do sheep give out on Halloween?

Candy baaaaas

What do you call a bear with no teeth?

A gummy bear

What's the best day to eat Halloween candy?

On Chews-day

Knock, knock.

Who's there?

Maple.

Maple who?

I maple the door off its hinges if I don't get any candy soon!

What kind of candy is never on time?

Choco-late

What did the student give to her teacher on Halloween?

A candy apple

Knock, knock.

Who's there?

Oswald.

Oswald who?

Oswald my Halloween candy without chewing.

—Gulp!

What is a playground's favorite candy?

Recess pieces

Why was the candy apple so excited on Halloween?

He was going to see his Granny Smith.

Knock, knock.

Who's there?

Witch.

Witch who?

Witch lollipop would you like?

What is a rabbit's favorite candy?

Lolli-hops

What treat do eye doctors give out on Halloween?

Candy corneas

Knock, knock.

Who's there?

Candy.

Candy who?

Candy cow jump over de moon?

What has teeth but can't eat Halloween candy?

A comb

Knock, knock.

Who's there?

Atomic.

Atomic who?

I have atomic ache from all the candy.

What is a math teacher's favorite kind of candy?

Measure-mints

Knock, knock.

Who's there?

Alibi.

Alibi who?

Alibi you a box of candy if you open the door.

How can you spell *candy* with only two letters?

C and Y

TRICKS AND TREATS

Knock, knock.

Who's there?

Thor.

Thor who?

Thorry, wrong door.

What runs around a haunted house and never stops?

A fence

Knock, knock.

Who's there?

Apple.

Apple who?

Apple on the door, but it won't open!

Knock, knock.

Who's there?

Handsome.

Handsome who?

Handsome of that candy over, please. I'm hungry!

Why did the boy carry a clock and a bird on Halloween?

He was going tick-or-tweeting.

Knock, knock.

Who's there?

Ice cream.

Ice cream who?

Ice cream when I'm scared—don't you?

What's the best game to play on Halloween?

Hide-and-shriek

Knock, knock.

Who's there?

Lettuce.

Lettuce who?

Lettuce in, please!

How do you find out the weather on Halloween?

Look out the window

Knock, knock.

Who's there?

Goat.

Goat who?

Goat to the door and find out!

Knock, knock.

Who's there?

Avery.

Avery who?

Avery nice person is knocking on the door. You should come say hi.

What did the police officer say to the two boys playing in the cemetery?

"You boys could be in grave danger."

Knock, knock.

Who's there?

Harry.

Harry who?

Harry up and open the door!

Knock, knock.

Who's there?

Peg.

Peg who?

Peg your pardon—I've got the wrong door.

Knock, knock.

Who's there?

Wooden shoe.

Wooden shoe who?

Wooden shoe like to know who's knocking on your door?

What do you call your neighborhood on Halloween?

Treat Street

Knock, knock.

Who's there?

A little boy.

A little boy who?

A little boy who can't reach the doorbell.

Knock, knock.

Who's there?

Allison.

Allison who?

Allison for someone to come to the door, but I don't hear anyone coming.

Knock, knock.

Who's there?

Gargoyle.

Gargoyle who?

If you gargoyle with salt water, your throat will feel better.

Knock, knock.

Who's there?

Tank.

Tank who?

You're welcome.

On Halloween, what gets lots of answers but no questions?

A doorbell

Knock, knock.

Who's there?

Howl.

Howl who?

Howl you know unless you open the door?

Knock, knock.

Who's there?

Wanda.

Wanda who?

Wanda go trick-or-treating?

What did the prince say on Halloween?

Rapunzel, Rapunzel, let down your scare!

Knock, knock.

Who's there?

Doris.

Doris who?

Doris closed. That's why I'm knocking.

Knock, knock.

Who's there?

Goblin.

Goblin who?

Goblin your candy will give you a tummyache.

Knock, knock.

Who's there?

Ben.

Ben who?

Ben knocking on this door for an hour and no one's given me candy.

Knock, knock.

Who's there?

Peas.

Peas who?

Peas open the door. It's so cold outside!

Mom: Did you thank Mrs. Smith for the lovely Halloween party she gave?

Audrey: No, Mom. The girls leaving before me thanked her, and Mrs. Smith said, "Don't mention it." So I didn't.

Knock, knock.

Who's there?

Isadore.

Isadore who?

Isadore bell here? I'm tired of knocking.

Knock, knock.

Who's there?

Water.

Water who?

Water you waiting for? Let me in.

Knock, knock.

Who's there?

T. rex.

T. rex who?

There's a *T. rex* trick-or-treating and you want to know its name?

One day a bat left to get food and returned with a huge bump on his head.

First bat: What happened?

Second bat: You see that tree over there?

First bat: Yes.

Second bat: Well, I didn't.

Knock, knock.

Who's there?

Heywood, Hugh, and Harry.

Heywood, Hugh, and Harry who?

Heywood Hugh Harry up and open the door?

Knock, knock.

Who's there?

Ivan.

Ivan who?

Ivan to go trick-or-treating!

What does an elephant say on Halloween?

Trunk-or-treat!

Knock, knock.

Who's there?

Theodore.

Theodore who?

Theodore is shut—please open it.

What is dark but made by light?

A shadow

Knock, knock.

Who's there?

Weirdo.

Weirdo who?

Weirdo you think you're going?

Knock, knock.

Who's there?

Isolate.

Isolate who?

Isolate to the Halloween party—I almost missed it!

Why did Humpty Dumpty have a great fall?

Because Halloween is his favorite holiday

Knock, knock.

Who's there?

Arthur.

Arthur who?

Arthur any candy bars left?

        Knock, knock.

        Who's there?

        Olive.

        Olive who?

        Olive my Halloween candy is gone already!

Knock, knock.

Who's there?

Twig.

Twig who?

Twig-or-tweat!

WEREWOLF WISECRACKS

Knock, knock.

Who's there?

Logan.

Logan who?

Logan see if there's a full moon outside—the dogs are howling!

What do you call a werewolf with no sense of direction?

A were-am-I-wolf

Why do werewolves have fur coats?

Because they don't look as good in denim jackets

How do werewolves greet each other?

"Howl's it goin'?"

What happened when Dracula met the werewolf?

They fought tooth and nail.

Why don't werewolves get cold?

They're always in fur coats.

What is a werewolf's least favorite dance?

The tangle

Where do werewolves go on vacation?

Howl-ywood

How does the werewolf keep his fur neat?

He uses a scare-brush.

What did one werewolf say to another?

"Let's go catch some fast food."

Why did the werewolf cross the road?

He was chasing the chicken!

What happened when the werewolf swallowed a clock?

He got ticks.

Rachel: Did you hear about the comedian at the werewolf party?

Pedro: No, what happened?

Rachel: She had them howling all night!

What do you call a werewolf with a fever?

A hot dog

What do you call a hairy beast that is lost?

A where-wolf

What did the werewolf say when someone stepped on his foot?

"Aoooowwwwww!"

What side of a werewolf has the most fur?

The outside

ANIMAL ANTICS

What does every tarantula wish she had?

A hairy godmother

Knock, knock.

Who's there?

Bat.

Bat who?

Bat you can't guess.

What do you call it when it rains cats?

A down-purr

What is a spider's favorite picnic food?

Corn on the cobweb

What works in the circus, meows, and does somersaults?

An acro-cat

Gordon: Why did you put that spider in my bed?

Lars: Because I couldn't find a frog.

Why was the owl a great investigative reporter?

He was always asking. Who? Who? Who?

What do you call a dog magician?

A labracadabrador

What animal flies around schools on Halloween night?

The alpha-bat

What is a cat's favorite meal?

Mouse-a-roni and cheese

Knock, knock.

Who's there?

Baby owl.

Baby owl who?

Baby owl see you later or baby owl just call you.

Why did the spider build a web?

To search it for information

What is a cat's favorite color?

Purr-ple

How do bats fly in the rain?

They use their wing-shield wipers.

What subject do owls like to study?

Owl-gebra

What did the spider do when he got a new car?

He took it out for a spin.

Knock, knock.

Who's there?

Detail.

Detail who?

Detail of de cat is on de end.

Why did the owl say "woof"?

She was learning a new language.

Where do cats go to look at fine art?

The mew-seum

How are bats like false teeth?

They come out at night.

What do spiders eat in France?

French flies

What do you call a cat drinking lemonade?

A sourpuss

Knock, knock.

Who's there?

Moo.

Moo who?

Make up your mind! Are you a cow or an owl?

Cary: I know someone who thinks he's an owl.

Mary: Who?

Cary: Make that two people.

Where do cats record their notes?

On scratch paper

Why did the spider leave home?

It wanted to change websites.

Knock, knock.

Who's there?

Me.

Me who?

You sure have a funny-sounding cat.

What are spider webs good for?

Haunted houses

**Why was the cat afraid
of the tree?**

Because of its bark

What is an owl's favorite soft drink?

Hoot beer

Knock, knock.

Who's there?

Howdy.

Howdy who?

Howdy cat get outside?

How do spiders learn definitions?

*They use Web-ster's
dictionary.*

Knock, knock.

Who's there?

Indonesia.

Indonesia who?

Spiders make me weak Indonesia.

What do bats do for fun?

They like to hang out with their friends.

What did the cat say when he stubbed his toe?

"Me-ow!"

What animal is best at hitting a baseball?

A bat

Diner: There's a fly in my soup!

Waiter: Don't worry. The spider on the bread will take care of it.

Why was the cat so small?

Because she only drank condensed milk

What is it called when a cat wins a dog show?

A cat-has-trophy

What do bats do for exercise?

Acro-bat-ics

What does a spider work on while using a computer?

Her website

Knock, knock.

Who's there?

Zany.

Zany who?

Zany body seen the cat?

What is an owl's favorite dessert?

Mice cream

Knock, knock.

Who's there?

Don.

Don who?

Don scream, but there's a spider by your foot.

Jim: Someone called you an owl today.

Paige: Who? Who?

Jim: Now I see why!

Why did the fly fly?

Because the spider spied her

What's another name for a cat's home?

A scratch pad

How do baby bats learn how to fly?

They just wing it.

Knock, knock.

Who's there?

Isabelle.

Isabelle who?

Isabelle on the cat's collar?

What keeps bats going?

Batteries

What do you call the event where spiders get married?

A webbing

What do you call two spiders that just got married?

Newly-webs

Knock, knock.

Who's there?

Who.

Who who?

I didn't know you spoke Owl!

What kind of car has whiskers and purrs?

A Cat-illac

Mother Cat: Go to bed, please.

Kitten: But I don't want to!

Mother Cat: That's enough of that cat-itude.

What do you call an eight-sided cat?

An octo-puss

What does a spider do when he gets angry?

He goes off the wall.

Knock, knock.

Who's there?

Owl.

Owl who?

Owl aboard!

What is a black cat's favorite school subject?

Hiss-tory

What happened when the cat ate a ball of yarn?

She had mittens.

What did the cat say after telling a funny joke?

"I'm just kitten."

Knock, knock.

Who's there?

Spider.

Spider who?

In spider everything, I still like you.

Lou: What is the difference between a fly and a bat?

Mom: I don't know. What?

Lou: A bat can fly, but a fly can't bat!

What did one spider ask the other spider?

"Could you connect me to the web?"

Why did the cat lie on the computer?

To keep an eye on the mouse